Disney's
American Frontier #5

JOHNNY APPLESEED
AND THE
PLANTING OF THE WEST
A Historical Novel

By Gina Ingoglia
Illustrations by Charlie Shaw
Cover illustration by Dave Henderson

DISNEP PRESS

NEW YORK

Look for these other books in the
American Frontier series:

Calamity Jane at Fort Sanders

Davy Crockett and the Creek Indians

Davy Crockett and the Highwaymen

Davy Crockett and the King of the River

Davy Crockett and the Pirates at Cave-in Rock

Davy Crockett at the Alamo

Sacajawea and the Journey to the Pacific

FIRST EDITION
1   3   5   7   9   10   8   6   4   2

Library of Congress Catalog Card Number: 92-52978
ISBN: 1-56282-258-6/1-56282-259-4 (lib. bdg.)

Consultant: Jack Larkin, Chief Historian
Old Sturbridge Village
Sturbridge, Massachusetts

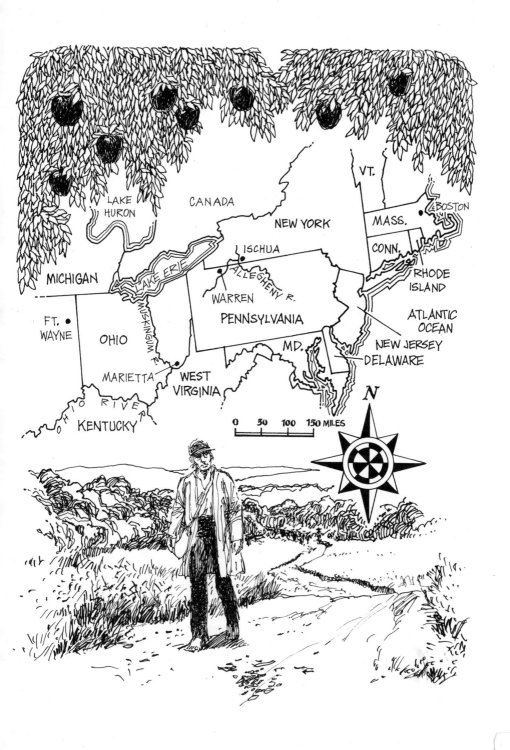

CHAPTER 1

Listen to this, Nat," said Johnny. "Here's another one of those newspaper articles I was telling you about! It says more than one hundred young men leave Boston every year. By 1800—just six years from now—a *thousand* more will have left! They're all heading for the West to seek new lives and fortunes."

Johnny put down the paper and looked at his younger brother Nat, who was thirteen.

"I've decided to go, too!" Johnny said. His dark eyes were bright with excitement. "It's all settled. I've been thinking about it for over a month now. I'm twenty years old, and it's time I was out on my own."

Nat turned his back to Johnny and stared out the open window overlooking the tiny garden. He didn't want his brother to see how upset he was by the thought of his leaving.

On the other side of a low stone wall, the late afternoon sun shone down upon the apple trees in the family's small apple orchard. The July air was so humid, it didn't even cool off after the sun went down. Nat had felt as if the summer would never end. And now he'd just heard the worst news of his life.

His favorite brother was leaving! It would be awful with Johnny gone, Nat thought. He didn't know how he'd stand it.

"Just how far west will you go?" Nat asked glumly. He watched as a squirrel scratched around the wilted flowers.

"I'm not sure yet," said Johnny. "At first, I thought I'd head for western Pennsylvania Country. But the government's opening up lots of land in the Ohio Country. There's all kinds of open space out there, and I mean to live in some of it!"

Johnny walked over to Nat, turned him around, and looked him square in the face.

"How would you like to go with me?" he asked.

"Really?" said Nat brightly. "*Me?*"

"Sure," answered Johnny. "You don't think I'd leave you behind, do you? I'm sure to need help getting started, and you and I would make a fine team. We'll have a great adventure out west, Nat! Tonight at supper, we'll talk to Mama and Pa about it."

That night at supper, Lucy Chapman shook her head as she handed a bowl of applesauce to her son.

"I'm sorry, Johnny," she said. "But I think Nat is too young to go with you, traveling all that way—he's only thir-teen!"

"I finished with school last season, Mama," said Nat. "I'd be getting a job, anyway. And it sure is boring here in Longmeadow. I'd like to go someplace new."

"I'll watch out for him, Mama," said Johnny. "We'll get along just fine."

Nathaniel Chapman listened to his oldest son and tapped a newspaper lying open next to his plate. "I read this article you showed me about adventurous boys heading west," he said. "You seem to have neglected part of the story."

He propped his glasses on his nose, cleared his throat, and read aloud: "There, amid fever, chills, and savages, the young men eke out a mere existence, while the more fortunate fellows who remain behind in the Boston vicinity live in peace and plenty."

Johnny's sister Patty, a little girl with long blond braids, stopped nibbling a slice of hot bread.

"What's that mean, Pa?" she asked.

Her brother Abner, who was eleven years old, spoke up.

"It's just some newspaper writer's fancy way of saying lots of people get sick out west," he explained, "and that it's a hard life and that they'd be better off staying safe and sound at home.

"It also says the place is full of wild Indians," he added. "Johnny'd better watch out or he's gonna get scalped!"

The little girl stopped eating. She blinked and sniffed a few times, looked at Johnny, and began to cry.

"Now see here, Abner," his father said sternly. "You're getting Patty all upset. This kind of talk won't do at all!"

Johnny put down his fork and looked across the table at Abner.

"No," he said in a low and steady voice. "It won't do. It won't do to talk this way about the Indians. They aren't savages as the paper says. They're people, Abner, just like us. If we treat them right, they'll treat us right."

"You can't be sure—" began Abner.

"I am sure!" said Johnny. "I'm sure about the Indians, and I'm sure about going out west."

"And I'm sure I'd like to go along with him!" added Nat.

Johnny looked at his family. He'd miss them all— especially Mama. She loved him as if he were her own son.

He hardly remembered his real mother, who had died when he was only two. Lucy had been his mother since he was six, and he felt proud to call her Mama.

"I don't see what's wrong with staying in Massachusetts," she said to Johnny. "You've done so well at school here in Longmeadow. Why, I'll bet you could even make it to college, Johnny. There are plenty of opportunities for a smart young man such as yourself here in Boston."

"I agree Boston is a fine place for some people," said Johnny. "But I want to go somewhere else. It would be an adventure to move west, to unknown lands where people are settling down and starting up new lives."

"What will you do there, Johnny?" she asked.

"I can't say for sure right now," he answered. "But after I get there I'll find out. I know something's out there—just waiting for me!"

Johnny got up. Standing straight and tall, he spoke to his father.

"I can make it work, Pa," he said. "Nat'll be safe with me. We'll build our own cabin and hunt and fish and grow some crops. I'll work hard and try to make something of myself. And when I start earning money, I'll send some back home to help you out."

Johnny's father kept on eating and didn't answer. Johnny could see the man was deep in thought.

"I have a cousin, Benjamin Chapman," Nathaniel finally said. "He settled his family out in western New York, in Ischua. That's on the Allegheny River, near the Pennsylvania border. We were close as boys; I know Ben'll help you out. You could stay with him for the winter before going farther west. It wouldn't make sense to write him that you're coming; you'll probably get there before the letter arrives.

"You'd better get going soon if you want to get there before winter hits," he continued. "It's a long way—over three hundred miles. You'll have to work your way cross-country on the rivers, and you'll also have lots of walking to do. It'll take you at least two months to make the trip."

He smiled at young Nat, his namesake. "If it's all right with your mother, you can go with Johnny," he said.

"Can I, Mama?" asked Nat, eagerly.

His mother thought it over. At first she looked sad and worried, but then she smiled.

"You may go," she said. "With both Ben and Johnny watching out for you, you should be safe."

CHAPTER 2

Johnny and Nat left two weeks later and worked their way westward across Massachusetts and northern Connecticut, south along the Housatonic River. There, in exchange for their passage, they loaded and unloaded cargo on a long flat-bottomed riverboat. The boat was pushed along the water by men using long poles. A short, wiry man named Culver Pennypacker was in charge. All the men called him Captain.

On a late afternoon, after they'd been on the river for more than a week, Johnny and Nat were relaxing on the open deck. It had been a long, hard day. They'd had to unload and take on heavy cargo at nine stops, and they were tired.

Johnny pushed against the railing, stretching his sore arm muscles. He looked out at the woods bordering the river.

Every mile or so, Johnny saw a little log cabin nestled in a clearing. Often, excited children ran outdoors, waving and shouting to the passing boat.

Along the shore, some loggers were hard at work. The ringing of iron axes echoed back and forth across the water as the burly men chopped wood. Occasionally someone shouted *"Timberrr!"* as a warning to anyone nearby that a giant tree was ready to fall.

The loggers skidded heavy logs into the river, down slopes dug into the ground. The logs bumped against one another as they floated on the river, heading for the nearest sawmill.

The boat rounded a bend, and one of the crew spotted trouble right away.

"Logjam, Captain!" he shouted. "And we're headed right for it!"

Hundreds of logs, wedged together, blocked the boat's way. Loggers were skillfully balanced on the logs, trying to break up the jam with long poles.

"More logs behind us!" Pennypacker shouted. "If we get caught in the middle of this jam, we'll be ground to a pile of splinters!"

Ahead, the loggers struggled to clear the way. As the boat approached the jam, some of the logs worked themselves loose. A path scarcely wider than the boat opened up.

"Yahoo!" shouted Nat. "We'll just make it!"

He leaned far over the edge and watched the boat inch its way past the logs.

"Careful there, young feller," Pennypacker warned Nat. "We're not clear of danger yet!"

The warning had hardly left Pennypacker's mouth when several logs crashed into the side of the boat. The boat lurched, and Nat pitched headfirst into the river. He hit the side of a log, then disappeared under it.

"Nat!" shouted Johnny. He threw himself into the water after his brother.

"Man overboard—starboard side!" Pennypacker shouted.

At the spot where he last saw Nat, Johnny dived beneath the water. Above him, floating logs blocked out the sunlight. He could hardly see. Johnny peered through the dark shadows, but Nat was nowhere in sight.

As Johnny frantically searched, thoughts raced through his head: He was responsible for Nat. He'd assured Mama and Pa he'd take care of his brother. Johnny knew their hearts would break if anything happened to Nat....

Johnny broke through the surface, took a deep breath, and dived back down. Rays of sunlight now lit up the bottom of the river, and Johnny spotted Nat lying right beneath him. He quickly reached down and grabbed Nat by his shirt. Using his last bit of strength, Johnny pulled his brother to the surface.

"There they are!" shouted Pennypacker. Several crewmen jumped into the water and helped Johnny pull Nat back to the boat. Pennypacker lifted Nat onto the boat and laid him face-down.

"He hit his head on a log," Pennypacker said. "He's out cold."

A little stream of water trickled from Nat's mouth. After a moment, he opened his eyes.

"Nat," asked Johnny, "are you all right?"

Nat blinked and coughed hard a few times, then looked up at Johnny.

"What happened?" he asked in a dazed voice.

"You fell overboard, got yourself knocked out, and took a little underwater swim," said Pennypacker. "Your brother here fished you out!"

"Knocked out!" said Nat. "You mean I was unconscious?"

"Cold as a mackerel," said Pennypacker.

"I always wondered what that would be like," said Nat as he sat up and rubbed his head.

"Well, now you know," said Pennypacker. "And you'd better thank your brother—you almost drowned!"

"Thanks, Johnny," said Nat. "I'm really sorry—I should have been more careful."

Johnny smiled. He didn't want Nat to see how frightened he'd been.

"It's all right," he said. "You just gave me a chance to practice my swimming!"

CHAPTER 3

One afternoon later that week, it was time for Johnny and Nat to go ashore and continue their journey on foot.

"I'm sorry to see you boys go," Pennypacker said. "For skinny fellers, you sure can heft cargo around! Where're you off to?"

"We're heading for the Allegheny River," said Johnny. "Our father's cousin has a cabin out in southwestern New York—in Ischua. We're going to spend the winter with him."

"There's not much out there on that part of the river," said Pennypacker. "You've got a long trip ahead of you. Are you sure your cousin lives there?"

"Isn't there a town?" asked Nat.

"That's what I'm saying," said Pennypacker. "There isn't any town yet. Just a few settlers here and there.

"Tell you what," he continued. "The boat's tied up here until tomorrow. Sleep aboard tonight, then you can get a good fresh start in the morning."

During the night, the frost of the season chilled everybody's bones. But by morning, it was warmer, and after a big breakfast of meat, gravy, hot corncakes, and steaming coffee, Johnny and Nat were ready to go.

"Well, boys," said Pennypacker, "I hope you find your relatives."

He handed a small sack to Johnny.

"Take these," he said. "Apples. They'll help keep you going."

"Thank you," said Johnny. "You've been very good to us. With the good Lord's help, we'll meet again someday."

Pennypacker patted Johnny on the back.

A cool breeze rippled the water, slapping it against the side of the boat.

"I just hope we find Uncle Ben before it snows," said Johnny.

Pennypacker nodded and looked at the sky.

"I think you've got a little time yet," he said. "We're having a real nice Indian summer. You're lucky. It's usually lots colder by now."

Johnny and Nat hiked across New Jersey and into upper Pennsylvania. By early October, they had reached the Allegheny River. They built a dugout canoe from the trunk of a tree and, paddling with long flattened-out pieces of bark, made their way up toward Ischua.

Rays of autumn sunlight filtering down through the treetops lit up the golden-leafed sugar maples and fiery red sumac. Amid these splendid trees, blue-gray pines and dark green hemlocks stood tall and straight, waiting for winter.

"It's sure pretty around here," said Nat. He took a deep breath of the crisp air. "Just as pretty as Massachusetts in the fall."

"We're lucky the weather has held out," said Johnny. "It's taking us longer to get to Ischua than Pa thought."

"What if we don't find the cabin?" asked Nat. "What'll we do then?"

"If we follow the river," said Johnny, "we should be all

right." He looked around. Pennypacker had been right; there wasn't a soul in sight.

Every now and then, they would come across a fur trapper. Each one told Johnny and Nat the same thing—Ischua was still miles ahead on the river. Nat was getting worried. Is *this* what they'd come so far for?

Then, early one morning a few weeks later, they heard a rifle shot.

"Johnny!" said Nat. "Sounds like somebody's huntin' in the woods."

Johnny sniffed the air. "I smell smoke," he said. "I'll bet there's a cabin close by. Let's go ashore and see if we can find it."

They paddled over to the edge of the river and pulled the canoe onto the bank. Then they headed in the direction of the rifle shot. Most of the ground was easy to cover. Here and there the water cut into the land, and they had to be careful not to step into a deep watery hole.

"Keep a sharp eye out for the cabin," said Johnny. "It should be around here somewhere." Another rifle shot cracked in the woods. A man's deep voice carried through the trees: "Corey, go tell Ma there's a rabbit for supper!"

"Whoopee!" shouted Nat. "I think we found 'em!"

A large dog bounded from the thicket, barking excitedly and wagging its tail. It ran in circles around Nat, sniffing at him and nipping at his trousers. In a few moments a little boy appeared, dangling a dead rabbit from one hand. He looked at Johnny and Nat, surprised to see people in the woods.

"Here he is, Pa," the boy called loudly into the trees. "I got Rowdy!"

He turned to Nat. "Sorry 'bout that," he said as he

pulled his dog off Nat. "Ol' Rowdy's sort of skittish. He gets all het up when he sees people, which ain't too often round here. I'm Corey Palmer—who're you?"

Before Nat could answer, Corey's father emerged from the woods, carrying a long rifle.

"Howdy," he said, extending his hand to Johnny. "I'm Caleb Palmer. You're a surprise—I didn't know anyone else lived in these parts."

Johnny introduced himself and Nat.

"We don't live here," he explained. "We're looking for our father's cousin, Benjamin Chapman. Have you heard of him?"

"Heard of him!" said Caleb. "I *know* him!"

Johnny and Nat smiled at each other. Things were looking up.

"Haven't seen Ben for a couple of years," said Caleb. "I suppose he's still in the same place. He and Addy've got a pack of young'uns, you know. Don't know as they've got much room for more family...."

"We mean to stay with them just for the winter," explained Johnny. "We'll be heading back to Pennsylvania in the spring."

"How far away do they live?" asked Nat.

"Real close," said Caleb. " 'Bout seven miles south."

"If we get going," said Johnny to Nat, "we'll make it by sundown."

"Doubt it," said Caleb. "It's not so easy getting there. Lots of fast-moving streams. Some take a while to cross—the rocks are mighty slippery. It gets pretty hilly, and the woods are thick with tangles and thorns." He gave them directions on how best to reach Ben's cabin.

"Good luck, boys," he said. "If you ever need any help, we're here. Don't forget, when you get to the rise, you'll see Ben's cabin down in the valley. It's in a clearing, smack-dab in the middle of a hickory grove. If you can't spot it, you've gone too far south!"

Caleb turned out to be right; they didn't make it by sundown. The trip through the unfamiliar woods took them almost two days. During that time, they finished Pennypacker's apples and slept on the ground, nestled in piles of fallen leaves.

They reached the rise by early afternoon on the second day. The sun was bright, but the air was cool. The warm Indian summer days were just about over.

Johnny set down his pack, shaded his eyes from the sun, and scanned the wide valley for the cabin. Almost at once he found it—right where Caleb said it would be.

"There it is," he said, pointing out the cabin to his brother.

"We made it!" said Nat. "I'm starved—I sure could use something nice and hot in my belly. Let's go."

Johnny wasn't listening to Nat. He kept staring at the cabin.

"There's no smoke," he said. "On a chilly day like this you'd think they'd have a fire going."

They climbed down to the valley floor and hiked through the quiet grove of hickories. Except for the chirping of busy nuthatches, there was no sign of life among the tall shaggy-barked trees.

"Sure is quiet round here," whispered Nat. "Sorta like being in church."

They reached the clearing and saw the cabin.

"Halloo!" called Johnny. He walked toward the house,

with Nat following close behind. The land, once cleared, was now overgrown. In some places, straggly weeds reached their knees.

"Johnny, " Nat said, his voice a bit shaky. "I don't think anybody lives here anymore."

The door to the cabin hung crooked and partly open. Inside, there was one room with a large stone fireplace. A ladder, leaning against the opening to a high loft, led to sleeping quarters under the roof. Dried leaves and gathered twigs littered the pounded dirt floor. Except for a broken chair lying on its side and a worn-out broom propped in the corner, the room was empty and very cold.

"They must have moved on," said Johnny.

There were tears in Nat's eyes.

Johnny patted his brother's shoulder. "Don't worry," he said. "We'll be all right. But there's a lot to do."

Johnny squatted on the floor, opened his large pack, and emptied it next to him. He pulled out two blankets; fish lines and hooks; tin cups and plates; a frying pan and large pot; knives, forks, and spoons; a sharp hatchet; and two small metal tinderboxes for starting fires.

He handed the pot and fishing gear to Nat.

"See if you can find something to eat while I chop some wood," he said. "It'll be a real race getting this place in shape by dark!"

Johnny and Nat got right to work, and by sunset, things seemed a lot better. A crackling fire warmed the clean-swept floor, and the door hung straight, shutting out the cold night air. Freshly chopped wood stood neatly stacked at one end of the room. In the loft, mounded dry leaves, covered with the blankets from home, made a roomy, comfortable bed.

Johnny knelt in front of the fire, cleaning a brook trout on an old board left behind by the Chapmans.

"This won't be so bad after all," said Nat as he nibbled on some berries and nuts he'd picked in the woods. "We'll get along just fine."

Johnny, his face serious, looked at Nat.

"Listen to me, Nat," he said. "Now that we're a bit settled, I have to tell you something. We can't survive living like this. We'll never make it through the winter. I've got to get us some real supplies. I'll leave first thing in the morning, and I'll be back as soon as I can."

"You're *leaving* me here?" cried Nat. "I don't want to stay here all by myself. I want to go with you."

"I can travel faster alone," said Johnny, "and I want to beat the snow. I'll go back to the Palmers'. Caleb said he'd help us out if we needed it."

Nat still looked upset.

"You'll be safe," said Johnny. "You won't go hungry with all the berries and nuts around. And there's bound to be plenty more fish in the stream. Just don't go too far from the cabin!"

CHAPTER 4

Johnny started off very early the next morning, heading north to the Palmers' cabin. The wind started to pick up, rustling the remaining leaves in the trees. The only other sounds he heard were dry leaves on the forest floor crunching beneath his feet.

By sunset, Johnny was about two hours away from the Palmers' place. He camped for the night and had a supper of freshly caught fish and ripe berries.

Johnny found a place to sleep inside a big hollow tree. He could tell that the hollow had once been an animal's den, most likely that of a black bear. The animal had lined the den floor with moss, grasses, and leaves. It looked like a fine place to spend the night, so Johnny crawled inside. He blocked the opening with his heavy knapsack to keep out the cold night air, and within minutes he was asleep.

At dawn, Johnny was awakened by the sound of leaves being crunched. He opened his eyes just in time to see his knapsack disappear! Then a man's hand appeared in the tree hollow. It grabbed Johnny's sleeve and tugged gently on it.

Johnny quickly scrambled out of his resting place. He faced a long-haired man dressed in a deerskin shirt and

leggings. The man wore a long red-and-blue sash around his shoulders. The sash crossed in front of his chest and tied around his waist. A feather stuck straight up from his turban-like cap.

Without speaking, the man gave the knapsack back to Johnny. He pointed to the sky with his left hand and then wiggled his fingers.

Johnny looked up. The morning sky was dark gray. Johnny knew at once what the Indian man was trying to tell him. He was warning Johnny that it was going to snow.

"Thank you," said Johnny even though he didn't know if the Indian would understand his words. If Johnny had slept while it snowed, he could have frozen to death. This man had probably saved his life. Johnny was filled with gratitude.

Silently the Indian nodded to Johnny. Then he turned and left.

Johnny knew a bad storm would delay his return to Nat. He wouldn't be able to travel during a blinding snowfall; he might be stranded for days. Johnny hurried on his way and reached the Palmers' at midmorning, just as the snow began to fall.

Caleb and his wife, Sarah, gathered enough supplies and food to last Johnny and Nat a month or two. They packed dried apples, flour, salt, yeast, pickles, coffee, dried beans, beef, slabs of bacon, a wool blanket, candles, nails, strong rope, and a hammer. An hour later, a large wooden sled stood packed and ready to go.

"That snow's coming down hard," said Caleb. "I don't think you can leave now, Johnny. You'll never find your way."

"I have to go!" said Johnny. "Nat's out there all alone."

He opened the door and looked out. His heart sank. The

air was so thick with falling snow, he couldn't see ten feet away.

It snowed all afternoon and into the evening. Johnny spent the night with the Palmers, lying wrapped in a blanket in front of the fire. He woke up at dawn and was almost afraid to look outside. Was it still snowing too hard for him to leave? He got up and opened the cabin door. A gust of frigid air blew in his face—but the snow was tapering off.

Sarah came into the room to start breakfast.

"It looks as if you'll be able to leave soon, Johnny," she said. "But it's going to be quite a struggle getting the sled through all that snow."

Caleb and Corey came in from feeding the animals in the barn. They took off their coats and stamped the snow from their boots.

"Johnny," said Caleb. "After you get something to eat, you'd better get going. The sky looks pretty clear now. Let's hope it stays that way until you get back to your little brother."

"You people have been so generous to me," said Johnny. "I don't know what I would have done without your help."

"Glad we could do it," said Caleb. "Out here, things would be a sorry mess if neighbors didn't help each other."

Sarah gave Johnny a big breakfast of oatmeal, bacon, apple pie, corncakes, and coffee. While Johnny ate, Caleb pulled the sled outdoors and got a pair of snowshoes for him.

Johnny thanked the Palmers again and set off, wearing the snowshoes and pulling the loaded sled by a strong rope. The wooden runners slid easily across the snow, but as the hours passed, Johnny's arms grew tired, and the sled became harder to pull. It was going to take him much longer to get back than he had thought even if it didn't snow again.

As Johnny trudged through the woods, his breath turned

into puffs of mist as soon as it hit the air. His thoughts were of his little brother. Was Nat cold? Had he caught more fish? Had he found enough berries and nuts to eat?

Johnny was too worried about Nat to stop that night. The snow sparkled in the moonlight, and he could easily see where he was going. Every hour or so he stopped for just a few minutes to rest.

Johnny walked on all the next day, too. Late that afternoon, when he was still about ten hours from the rise, he felt a few snowflakes fall on his face. In minutes, snow was swirling around him. He had to stop and look for cover.

Shielding his eyes, Johnny looked around as best he could. The snow was falling thick and fast. If he didn't find shelter right away, he'd freeze. But then he spotted a cave, not ten feet away. Johnny couldn't believe his good fortune. He pulled the sled over to the cave and crawled inside, dragging the sled in after him.

Johnny looked around and saw the remains of an old fire and a little pile of dry leaves and wood. A message was scratched into the hard dirt with a stick: "Hope this wood warms your bones." Someone had left wood behind for the next traveler. Johnny recalled Caleb's words about neighbors helping each other in the wilderness. Now Johnny was being helped by someone he'd probably never even meet.

Johnny took out his tinderbox and quickly started a fire. As he did every night, Johnny read from the Bible that he always carried. He read by the flickering firelight, then knelt and said his prayers. He said a special prayer for Nat's safety. Gradually the fire began to warm him, and despite his worries about Nat, Johnny was soon fast asleep.

All night the snow kept falling. When Johnny awoke, it

was still dark outside. The fire had gone out, and he was cold and hungry. He groped his way over to the sled, and after fumbling a while with the rope, he managed to untie the pack. He put his hand into the opening and fished around for something to eat.

The first food Johnny found were some dried apples. He took a handful and ate them as he shivered in the icy darkness. He thought of his family back home and remembered that dinner when he'd felt so sure of himself. He'd told his mother that something was out west just waiting for him.

During these last weeks he'd often thought about why he was out here. What would he do in this new land, where it was a struggle just to find food and shelter?

The more Johnny thought, the more he knew what sort of thing he wanted to do. He wanted to make life easier for people to live in the wilderness. But how?

Johnny reached into the pack and grabbed another handful of dried apples. Suddenly he was struck by an idea. He knew exactly what he'd do.

CHAPTER 5

The snow had stopped by dawn, and Johnny started for
the cabin again. The sun was setting when he finally
reached the rise and peered down across the whitened
valley. He quickly spotted the cabin, smoke curling from the
chimney, the windows glowing with firelight. Johnny sighed
with relief. Nat was all right!

"Johnny!" shouted Nat when he spied his brother. "I was
so worried about you. With all that snow, I thought you might
be dead!"

"*I* was worried about *you*," said Johnny. He smiled at
Nat. "I see I needn't have bothered."

Johnny could hardly believe his eyes when he looked
around the cabin: an enormous bearskin rug lay in front of the
fireplace!

"How in the world did you get that?" asked Johnny.

"I went fishing the day after you left," Nat said. "It
started to snow, so I headed for home. But the snow started to
whirl around in the wind, and I couldn't see where I was
going. It was awful, Johnny. I was getting colder and colder.
And worst of all, I was walking in a circle—I kept ending up
in the same place! It was so hard to see, I fell in the stream."

"You fell in the stream?" asked Johnny.

"Yeah," said Nat. "Luckily, the water wasn't deep, and I pulled myself out. But I was soaking wet and colder than an icicle.

"Next thing I knew I felt myself being picked right off my feet! A man carried me back to the cabin, wrapped me up in our blankets, and dried my clothes in front of the fire. I was still shivering like mad, so the man felt my head and left to get this bearskin rug and some food. He put the rug on top of me and gave me a hot drink. It tasted terrible, but I stopped shivering. The whole time, he spoke not one word to me. He was an Indian, Johnny."

As Nat described the man to him, Johnny realized it was the same person who had warned him about the snowstorm. Now he'd saved Nat's life, too.

Listening to Nat's story confirmed for Johnny that helping others was the right thing for him to do. Since they'd arrived in Ischua, his and Nat's very lives had depended on other people's assistance. The Palmers, who hardly knew Johnny and Nat, had shared their own food and supplies. An unknown frontiersman, after camping in a cave, had thought enough to leave wood behind for the next person. And an Indian who happened to be passing by had saved *both* him and his brother. If Johnny couldn't repay these generous people, he would make every effort to help others survive.

"I know what I'm going to do out here, Nat," Johnny said when his brother had finished. "It came to me when I was eating dried apples in the cave. The frontier is a hard place to live, and people often have to help one another—just like we've been helped. The most important things out here are food and a place to live. And they are often pretty hard to get. I've decided to make sure people always have something to eat."

"How?" asked Nat.

"I'm going to see they all have apple trees," said Johnny. "And you can help me do it—for as long as you like."

"Apples?" asked Nat. "Really? That's your plan?"

Johnny nodded.

"Apples are the perfect food for pioneers," he explained. "You can eat them all year—we did at home. In the fall, you can eat apples right off the tree or bake them. You can press the juice from the bruised fruits to make cider...."

Nat made himself comfortable on the bearskin rug. Johnny sounded like he was just getting started.

"In winter," continued Johnny excitedly, "apples can last for months if they're stored in a cool cellar. You can eat all kinds of foods preserved in apple cider vinegar. And there's apple-blossom honey, dried apples, applesauce, apple butter, and—"

"Listen, Johnny," interrupted Nat, "I don't know about this. I thought we were out here to have an adventure. It seems to me I could be doing something else out here—something more exciting than helping you plant apple trees."

"I realize now that just being a part of this wild frontier is excitement enough," said Johnny. "It's important to help settle the frontier the best way we can. I think planting apple trees will help do that. And if there's one thing we know about, it's planting apple trees. After all, we're from the first place in America to grow them.

"And there's something else we shouldn't forget, Nat," Johnny said. "The winters here are so long that by spring everybody's in need of cheering up. And nothing beats the beauty of pink-and-white apple blossoms. They're pretty enough to make anyone a little happier."

Nat stretched out on the rug to think.

"How are you going to do all this?" he asked.

"In the spring we'll move to western Pennsylvania. We'll settle down where lots of people pass through on their way west," said Johnny.

"Then what?" asked Nat.

"I'll start apple-tree nurseries," said Johnny. "People can stop there and get young saplings to plant near their new homes. They can pay me what they can. If they haven't any money, I'll just give them away."

"Give them away!" said Nat. "Isn't that being too generous?"

"Not really," said Johnny. "It's in keeping with what Mama taught us from the Bible: 'All things whatsoever ye would that men should do to you—do ye even so to them.'

"Back home," continued Johnny, "every time a hungry tramp came to the door, Mama gave him something to eat. And lots of times it was apples!"

Nat thought a moment. Maybe he should help out Johnny after all.

"Well, tell me, Johnny," asked Nat, "what's a nursery? Is it like an orchard?"

"An orchard is where fruit trees grow for a long time," explained Johnny. "A nursery is a place to raise young trees. People take the baby trees to their homes to start their own orchards."

"What if folks are planning to travel a far distance from your nurseries?" asked Nat. "How will they be able to carry baby trees with them?"

"I'll give those people apple seeds," said Johnny, "so they can plant their own trees."

"Just where are you going to get all these apple seeds?" asked Nat.

"I don't know yet," said Johnny. "I'll figure that out when we get to Pennsylvania!"

CHAPTER 6

Johnny and Nat settled down for the winter in Ben's old cabin. One chilly morning at breakfast, Nat looked out the window and saw a man gathering nuts at the edge of the hickory grove.

"Johnny!" said Nat. "It's the man who helped me!"

In a few minutes, the Indian man was inside the cabin, and Nat was offering his guest a cup of hot coffee.

"This time," Nat said to Johnny, "*I* can give *him* something hot to drink!"

The Indian man put down a leather bag he was carrying and took the steaming cup from Nat's hand. Johnny gestured toward the table, and the three sat down.

"I wish we could talk to him," said Johnny.

After he finished his coffee, the man rose from his chair, picked up his leather bag, and dumped a pile of hickory nuts on the table. Then he nodded to Johnny and Nat and walked out the door, taking the empty bag with him.

He came back with a wooden bowl filled with corn flour. Keeping silent the whole time, he shelled and chopped the hickory nuts, then mixed the flour with water until it was pasty. He added the nuts and molded the corn paste into small

loaves. He placed the loaves in boiling water, and when they floated to the top, he gave them to Johnny and Nat to eat.

"I wonder why he's doing all this for us?" asked Nat.

"I guess he thinks we need help," said Johnny.

In the weeks that followed, Johnny and the Indian man learned how to communicate with each other. Each taught the other a little of his own language. Johnny learned that the Indian man's name was Red Hawk and that his people were farmers, living in the forest. Red Hawk taught Johnny all about plant medicine and how to use dried flowers, leaves, and roots to cure many ailments.

One day, after Red Hawk had left, Johnny told Nat, "Now I know why Red Hawk has taken such an interest in us. If I understood him correctly, some time ago, he was riding in the forest when his horse shied at a rattlesnake. He was thrown off the horse and broke his leg.

"A settler who was trapping beavers nearby found Red Hawk lying on the ground, made a splint out of tree branches, and set his leg. Then the settler helped Red Hawk get back on his horse."

"The settler saved Red Hawk's life," said Nat.

"That's right," said Johnny. "Because of all the fighting going on between Indian people and settlers, this man's act was very brave as well as kind. I think Red Hawk's being so kind to us is his way of thanking the settler who saved his life."

Johnny smiled. "But now," he said, "Red Hawk visits us because we have become friends."

CHAPTER 7

In late March, after the snows had finally stopped, it was time for Johnny and Nat to start out for Pennsylvania. They gave Red Hawk back his bearskin rug, and the three friends said good-bye with heavy hearts. They knew that the chances were very slim they would ever meet again.

Johnny and Nat packed the Palmers' sled with whatever provisions were left in the cabin. Except for their own gear and some food, they would give it all back to the Palmers.

On the morning Johnny and Nat left the cabin for good, the air was still frosty. But the snow was melting fast, and the streams ran free of ice.

Johnny and Nat dragged the sled through the woods over the half-frozen ground. Every now and then the sled's runners got stuck in patches of mud, but they were still able to make good time. They stopped at sundown and spent the night in a dry cave. By noon the next day, Johnny and Nat had arrived at the Palmers' cabin.

As they pulled the sled to the door, Rowdy scrambled up to greet them, his tongue dangling and his tail wagging a welcome.

The Palmers invited Johnny and Nat to join them for

dinner, and while they were all eating, Johnny and Nat told them about Red Hawk and about the winter they spent in Ben's old cabin.

"Where are you two headed now?" asked Caleb.

"To western Pennsylvania," said Johnny. "We're going back to the Allegheny River. Maybe we'll see a boat that will take us south."

"Johnny wants to give apple trees to everybody," said Nat.

"Apple trees?" asked Caleb, puzzled. "Why?"

Johnny explained his plan to the Palmers.

"I think it's a really good idea," said Corey. "I love apples!"

"I just want to be able to help other people as much as you all helped us," said Johnny.

When the brothers reached the Allegheny River, they found no boats, so they camped on the riverbank for two days.

"Let's build a raft," suggested Nat, "and float down the river by ourselves."

Johnny agreed, and they set to work. They cut down a pine tree; removed its branches; chopped the long, straight trunk into shorter logs; and lashed them together with rope. Then they found two long, sturdy limbs to serve as poles.

Early the next morning, they got under way. The current was swift and choppy, and sometimes it was hard to keep the fast-moving raft under control.

Johnny and Nat traveled downriver for three days. Each day was the same as the last: Before sundown, they poled the raft to the shore, built a fire, and caught a few fish. After supper, they slept beneath a leafy shade tree. At dawn, they gathered acorns still attached to low oak branches. Johnny boiled them and added some flour to make a sweet-tasting mush for breakfast. After the meal, they continued down the Allegheny.

On their fourth morning, before they climbed onto their raft, Johnny and Nat watched five covered wagons rumble down the bank to the water's edge. The first four wagons crossed without trouble. But when the fifth wagon neared the river, the horses refused to enter the swift current. A man climbed down from the wagon and tried to pull the horses into the water.

"Need any help?" called Johnny.

"Sure do," the man shouted back.

"You get back in the wagon and steer," Johnny told the man. "We'll try to take care of the horses."

Johnny and Nat each took hold of a horse's bridle, and speaking gently to the nervous animals, they led them into the river. With Johnny and Nat wading and swimming alongside them, the horses were able to pull the wagon to the opposite shore.

The man climbed down from the wagon seat. Five small redheaded children scrambled out after him. From behind the wagon, a woman appeared, carrying a small baby.

"Much obliged," said the man. He took off his hat and shook hands with Johnny and Nat. "Where're you fellers headin'?"

"We're not exactly sure," explained Johnny. "I'm looking for a place where lots of people pass through on their way west."

"Well, lots of folks pass through Warren," said the man. "We're headed that way. How about us giving you a ride? It'll be lots easier than poling your way down the river!"

Warren, Pennsylvania, was a new settlement. This made it an ideal place for Johnny to start his apple nurseries.

With the help of friendly neighbors, Johnny and Nat

built a large log cabin just a short distance from the settlement. Johnny planted a vegetable patch and kept a beehive out back. In exchange for a cow, Johnny and Nat worked several days for a farmer. They stored milk and butter inside a wooden springhouse that was built across a running brook. The milk was chilled by the cold water running beneath the springhouse. That way, the milk stayed fresh for days.

As soon as they were settled in, Johnny and Nat looked around for a place to start the nursery.

"What are we looking for?" asked Nat.

"I want terrain that's easy to clear, not full of big rocks or huge old trees," said Johnny. "And there should be a stream close by. Newly planted seeds need lots of water.

"The soil has to be easy to dig," Johnny went on, "with a good mixture of sand and clay in it. Clay keeps the soil from washing away, and sand keeps it from getting too sticky."

Several days later, Johnny and Nat were hiking a few miles away from their cabin, near a place called Brokenstraw Creek, when they came upon a broad open field that was fairly clear of large rocks. Only a few scrubby trees grew on it, and a stream ran nearby.

Johnny reached down and rubbed some soil between his fingers. It seemed the right mixture of clay and sand.

"This is the perfect spot for my nursery!" said Johnny.

The land belonged to a farmer who lived nearby. Johnny was in luck: The farmer wasn't planting the field and would let Johnny use it for his nursery. All he wanted in return was a good supply of apples for his family.

Johnny and Nat worked on the land all summer. They enclosed the grassy pasture with fallen logs and prickly brush to keep out wandering cattle. They chopped down the small trees and used pickaxes to dig out the stumps. Johnny and Nat used long, sharp scythes to rid the land of weeds and thickets. After the field was clear, the brothers plowed the land to break up the soil.

On a sunny September afternoon, the area was finally ready for planting. Johnny and Nat proudly looked at the result of their hard labor.

"There's room enough here for three thousand saplings," said Johnny. "We're all set!"

"All set except for the seeds," said Nat. "Where're they coming from?"

"I've got that all worked out," said Johnny. "Where would you expect to find zillions of apple seeds?"

"A cider mill?" guessed Nat.

"Exactly right!" said Johnny. "After the apples are pressed, the seeds are usually thrown out, so I'm hoping the mill owners will give them to me for free."

Johnny was right. The cider mill owners were happy to give him seeds. Johnny carried them home in large linen sacks, and that night he spent hours washing and sorting the seeds and spreading them out to dry. In the morning, he set aside some for his nursery. Then Johnny poured the rest into little deerskin bags so they would be ready to give away.

The cold weather set in, and fewer and fewer pioneering families passed Johnny's cabin. Finally, no more went by. The wagon trains would reappear when warm weather made traveling easier.

The following spring, Johnny planted his first nursery. With the help of summer sunshine and rain, the apple seeds sprouted. By fall, tiny saplings were growing in long, neat rows.

From time to time, Johnny left Warren to go traveling

through the countryside. Over the next two years, he planted more nurseries in other parts of western Pennsylvania. He either bought the land or leased it from farmers. After each nursery was planted, Johnny paid someone living nearby to look after the apple saplings and sell them. Then he made occasional visits back to the nurseries to check on the trees and collect his money.

Johnny's home in Warren became a resting place for pioneers weary from long months on the road. Whenever Johnny spotted a wagonload of travelers passing his cabin, he'd welcome them in for a rest.

"Stay as long as you like," Johnny would say. "There's plenty of room."

Johnny saw to it that each child drank lots of ice-cold milk from the springhouse and had a thick slice of bread covered with sweet, sticky honey from his hive. He also gave each child a shiny brown nut about the size of a walnut that he pulled from his pocket.

"They're called buckeyes," Johnny told the children, "and they come from horse chestnut trees. They're not good to eat, but if you carry them around in your pocket, they are supposed to bring you good luck!"

Before the families set out on their journeys again, Johnny gave them each a little leather bag full of apple seeds. It wasn't long before Johnny became known as the Apple Seed Man. But the name Johnny liked best was given to him by the children. They called him Johnny Appleseed.

CHAPTER 8

Around midnight one stormy night in late fall, someone rapped loudly on the cabin door.

Johnny opened the door to see a man wearing a large hat and black cape, soaking wet. The man's horse, burdened with heavy saddlebags, waited forlornly on the road.

"Will you give us shelter?" asked the man.

"Put your horse in the barn with the cow," said Johnny. "There's a blanket out there—use it to dry him off. Then come on back here. I'll make you some hot coffee."

"Thank you kindly," said the man. "But don't bother about the coffee. I don't drink it. Hot water will do just fine."

The man turned back into the rain, and Johnny closed the door.

"Hot water?" asked Nat. "Who'd want to drink *that?*"

"I'm sure we'll find out," said Johnny.

In a few minutes, the visitor was back. Johnny took his wet, heavy cape and draped it over a chair in front of the fire.

"Much obliged," said the man. He rubbed his hands together. "It certainly is a blessing to get out of that rain." He held out his hand to Johnny.

"I'm Judge John Young," he said. "I never expected to

get caught in a rain like this, and I am indeed grateful for your hospitality."

"Where are you from?" asked Johnny.

"Greensburg, Pennsylvania," said the judge. "About one hundred miles south."

"I have an apple-tree nursery near there," said Johnny.

"You must be Johnny Appleseed!" said the judge. "Many of the families in Greensburg bought trees from your nursery and started their own orchards with them. The folks back home said if I passed this way to tell you their apple trees are doing fine. It's a great thing you're doing, Johnny."

Johnny took a steaming kettle from the fire.

"Are you sure you want just hot water?" he asked the judge. "What about some vegetable soup instead? There's still some in the pot from our supper."

"Soup would be very fine," said the visitor. "I just didn't want to put you out."

Johnny heated up the soup and ladled it into a bowl. Nat sliced some brown bread for him.

"Why don't you drink coffee?" asked Nat.

Judge Young looked at Nat and smiled.

"Well, young man," he explained, " I believe in the world of the spirit. I have devoted my life to unselfish service and self-denial. I know coffee tastes mighty good, but if I make myself get along without certain worldly things, it is better for my soul."

"Uh-huh," said Nat, not understanding at all but trying to be polite.

"You sound like a religious man," said Johnny.

"Indeed I am," said Judge Young. He saw Johnny's Bible lying open on a table. "And I see you are one, too.

"I have some fine books about religion with me," the judge said, and he reached into his saddlebag. "Perhaps you'd like to see them?"

"I would indeed," said Johnny.

That night, while Nat and Judge Young slept, Johnny stayed up reading. At dawn, Judge Young awoke to find Johnny still reading by the fire.

"Judge Young," said Johnny, "these are wonderful books. You are fortunate to have them."

Judge Young smiled at Johnny.

"They're yours," he said. "You gave me food and a place to rest my head. I think that's a fair trade."

After breakfast, Judge Young saddled up his horse and prepared to leave.

"When you next visit your nursery in Greensburg," he said to Johnny, "don't forget to call on me." Then he shook hands with Johnny and Nat and went on his way.

After the judge's visit, Johnny put aside time every day to read his new books.

"Are you still reading that stuff?" asked Nat several weeks later. "You must have finished them by now."

"These books can never be finished, Nat," said Johnny. "They must be read again and again. They tell us how the real meaning of life is to serve others and God. Nothing else is important."

"You talk about religion all the time now," said Nat. "You haven't been the same since you got those books."

"I feel like a new man, Nat," said Johnny. "I'm seeing things clearly for the first time in my life."

"What things?" asked Nat.

"Remember I said the most important needs in the frontier were shelter and food?" asked Johnny. "Well, I was wrong. There's another need just as important—I'm going to help people feed their souls as well as their bodies."

"You sound like Judge Young," said Nat.

"I probably do," said Johnny with a little smile. "I've decided to spread the Word of God."

"You mean you'll be like a preacher?" asked Nat.

"I won't be a preacher appointed by a church," said Johnny. "But I think I can help out. There certainly aren't enough preachers out here in the wilderness!"

During the next months, when people stopped by Johnny's cabin, he fed them, preached a little, and read passages aloud from the Bible. Before his guests left, Johnny gave each of them a little bag of apple seeds.

One day in early spring, Nat came to Johnny and said, "What you're doing is good, but it isn't what *I* really want to do. I need to move on. I'd like to join a surveying team and help make maps of the new territories. There's a team leaving soon that's being led by a man named Moses Cleveland, and he's asked me to join them. It's exciting work, Johnny, and I want to do it."

Johnny smiled at his brother.

"I think it sounds like very good work, Nat," he said. "I was thinking of moving on myself. Lots of people are moving into the Ohio Country. I'd like to get out there soon and get my nurseries started. That way the saplings will be ready before many more settlers arrive."

CHAPTER 9

Within a month, Johnny and Nat were packed and ready to go their separate ways. Nat was the first to leave. The surveying party was off to lands south of Lake Erie called the Western Reserve. On the morning of Nat's departure, he and Johnny knelt together in the cabin and prayed.

"Dear Lord," said Johnny. "We ask for your blessings. Please protect thy servant Nat, who is about to embark on a new venture. May you protect him and guide him all his days. Amen."

Johnny walked with his brother to the doorway of the cabin.

"I'll miss you," they said at the same time.

"Johnny," said Nat. "I never really thanked you for taking me with you...."

Johnny put his arm around Nat. "You don't have to thank me," he said gently. "I'm the one who should be saying that to you. During these three and a half years on our own, you've always been a great help and a grand companion!"

Johnny gave Nat one last hug. "Godspeed, my dear brother," he said.

"Thank you," said Nat. "And good luck to you in Ohio—Mr. Johnny Appleseed!"

Johnny laughed, but he was very sad. He knew he and Nat were saying good-bye for good.

Johnny left the next morning. He began his long journey on foot, pulling a small wagon loaded with his pack and sacks of apple seeds. The pack held some roasted corn, dried apple slices, a chunk of cheese, salt, and a few beechnuts. There was also a hatchet and a sharp curved knife for pruning trees. His Bible was safely tucked inside his shirt.

A few weeks later, Johnny crossed the border of Pennsylvania and entered eastern Ohio. He wandered throughout the Ohio countryside for the rest of that year, and whenever he saw a likely spot, he planted a nursery.

Johnny didn't attend to much beyond his apple trees and his preaching. He stopped cutting his hair and let his beard grow long. After a while, his clothes became raggedy, and when his shoes wore out, he just went barefoot.

One day in early summer, Johnny was pulling his wagon along an old Indian trail through the southeastern Ohio woods when he came across a clearing. He saw a log cabin with wisps of smoke curling from its chimney and a tall ladder leaning against one of the cabin walls. The yard was empty except for a well with a wooden bucket hanging above it. A wooden post had been driven into the ground beneath a dogwood tree at the edge of the clearing. Outside the cabin door, a rooster and several brown hens pecked at kernels of corn that had been scattered on the dirt.

A neatly built split-rail fence enclosed part of the clearing around the cabin. One of the rails had fallen, leaving an opening in the fence.

Johnny heard a noise in the woods and turned to look. A brown-and-white cow, with a long rope hanging from her neck, was browsing among the trees and eating ferns.

"I know where you came from!" said Johnny. He led the cow back into the yard, tied the rope secure to the wooden post, and patted the cow's back.

"Whoever lives here will be glad to know you're back," said Johnny, and he went to the cabin door.

"Hello in there," called Johnny as he knocked. "Anybody home?"

"Praised be the Lord, Daniel," said a woman's soft voice. "Somebody's come."

Johnny opened the cabin door and looked inside.

The cabin was about fourteen feet wide and sixteen feet long. The pounded earth floor was covered by a worn, thin carpet. A small fire burned inside a stone fireplace at one end of the room. Four pine chairs and a cloth-covered table stood in front of the fireplace. Pale rays of sunlight filtered through a small window of greased paper. A spinning wheel for making thread and a loom for weaving cloth stood in the dim light.

Johnny saw a man and woman lying side by side on a wide bed pushed along one wall. The man's eyes were closed. His face, twisted with pain, was shiny with sweat. The woman looked pale and tired. She spoke weakly to Johnny.

"We are not well," she said. "Will you help us?"

Johnny stepped into the room and walked over to her.

"Of course," he said. "What's happened to you?"

"I'm Elizabeth Fletcher," the woman said. "Three weeks ago, my husband, Daniel, was fixing the roof. He fell off and cut his leg badly. I'm afraid it's infected—he's had a fever for the last week. And then our baby was born just three days ago...."

Johnny's eyes went to the wooden cradle next to the bed. A tiny baby slept inside.

"You had the baby all by yourself, without any help?" asked Johnny.

"Yes," said Elizabeth. "It wasn't easy, but I did it. But now I'm so weak, all I can do is keep the fire burning and throw some corn out the door for the chickens. This morning I noticed our cow's wandered off. Do you think you could find her?"

"She's back now," said Johnny. "I found her and tied her to the post."

Elizabeth gave a little smile.

"Things are looking better already," she said.

Johnny felt Daniel's feverish head and examined his leg. Elizabeth was right: Daniel's leg was badly infected.

"He's very hot," said Johnny. "We must bring his fever down. I noticed you have a dogwood tree in the yard. I think it will give us just what we need!"

Johnny cut pieces of bark from a branch of the tree, then put the pieces into a pot and poured boiling water over them. He set the pot down on hot ashes in the fireplace.

"Let this simmer until I get back," said Johnny. "I have to get something else."

Johnny walked into the shady woods behind the cabin and found a tall, drooping hemlock tree. He sliced off several small pieces of bark, and at the edge of the woods, he gathered bunches of bright yellow dandelions.

When Johnny got back to the Fletchers' cabin, he took the pot of dogwood-bark brew from the fireplace, poured the mixture into a tin cup, and held it to Daniel's lips.

"Drink this," said Johnny. "It will bring your fever down."

Daniel took a few sips and fell back exhausted.

Johnny gently washed Daniel's leg with water from the well. He put the hemlock bark into a pot and boiled it until the bark was soft. Then Johnny pounded it into a paste and spread it gently over Daniel's wound. He covered Daniel's leg with a clean cloth.

"Do you think he'll be all right?" asked Elizabeth.

"Yes, I do," said Johnny. "Hemlock bark will help his leg heal. And I've brought some dandelions for you."

"Thank you," said Elizabeth. "They're very pretty. We'd better put them in some water."

"I didn't bring them to look at," Johnny replied with a smile. "I'm going to make some dandelion tonic to help you get your strength back."

Johnny put the dandelion leaves into boiling water. After they brewed for a few minutes, he poured the dandelion-leaf tea into a tin cup for Elizabeth, who sipped it slowly.

"Where did you learn about plant medicine?" she asked Johnny.

"A man named Red Hawk taught me," said Johnny. He told Elizabeth a little about his winter in Ischua with Nat while she finished the tonic.

"I learned a lot from Red Hawk that winter," said Johnny.

"It's lucky for us you did," said Elizabeth.

Johnny stayed with the Fletchers for nearly a month. He fixed the roof and planted seeds in the vegetable patch. He washed their clothes and spread them along the fence to dry in the sun.

Each day, Daniel and Elizabeth grew stronger. Johnny cooked all their meals and helped Elizabeth with the baby.

Every night, after the chores were done, he read passages aloud from the Bible and talked about the glory of God.

Johnny cleared some land nearby and planted a small apple orchard for the Fletchers. He told Elizabeth and Daniel all about his nurseries.

"It takes a few years for the trees to bear fruit," said Johnny. "That's why I want to get out to the far edge of the wilderness before all the newcomers move in. By the time they get there, my saplings should already be grown and bearing fruit. The settlers can then buy their own trees from my nurseries and plant them for themselves. Soon after, they'll have apples—all ready for picking!"

"Right now, you're heading toward Marietta," said Daniel. "It's not the far edge of the wilderness, but lots of folks are settling around there. They can also tell you where other settlers are going.

"Follow the Indian trail to the Muskingum River," Daniel continued. "Marietta's about twenty miles downstream. You'll know you're close when you see old Fort Harmar. It's on a bluff where the Muskingum flows into the Ohio River."

"Marietta's a pretty busy place," said Elizabeth as she rocked the baby in her arms. "It's where we get our yearly supplies."

"There's something else Daniel and I want to tell you," she said. "We've decided to name the baby Chapman—after you."

"We'll call him Chappy," said Daniel. "And we'll tell him how Johnny Appleseed helped his family—and maybe even saved their lives."

CHAPTER 10

Johnny bid the Fletchers good-bye and followed the Indian trail to the Muskingum River. On the riverbank, Johnny did some chores for a man who lived nearby in exchange for two canoes. He lashed the canoes together, loaded his sacks of apple seeds into one of them, and put his dismantled wagon into the other. Then Johnny set off, paddling his strange-looking craft down the river.

Johnny reached the wide Ohio River and floated past Fort Harmar. The five-sided fort, built from the wood of poplar trees, stood silent on a high plain overlooking the river. The only sound came from atop a square tower, where the American flag snapped in the wind. Fort Harmar had been built to keep settlers from entering lands west of Marietta. But now that more land had opened up, the fort was no longer in use.

When Johnny arrived at Marietta's waterfront, he dragged the canoes onto the shore. Two boys, each about twelve years old, were standing nearby and came over to watch him.

"How would you like to help me put this wagon together?" asked Johnny.

"Sure," said one boy. "We're not doing anything."

After the wagon was assembled, they helped Johnny load the heavy sack of seeds into it.

"Thanks for your help," said Johnny. "The canoes are yours. Now you have something *fun* to do—you can take a ride on the river!"

Johnny pulled the wagon toward the center of town, passing by the houses and shops that lined the wide dirt road. A handsome clapboard house with a bay window caught his eye. A path bordered with wildflowers led the way to the front door.

Then Johnny saw something that took his breath away. An old apple tree, its branches heavy with ripening apples, stood in the front yard!

Johnny pulled the wagon up the path and stared at the tree. As he looked at it, an elderly man quietly came up beside him. He had gray hair, and his eyes had a cheery sparkle. He wore a black suit, a buttoned vest, and his trousers had sharp creases ironed into them. A black silk tie was neatly fastened under his stiff white collar.

"It's a beauty, don't you think?" asked the man in a deep, rich voice.

"It surely is," answered Johnny. "Do you live here? Is it your tree?"

"I do and it is," said the man. "My name is True— Doctor True," he said. "But some folks in town just call me Doc." He smiled and extended his hand to Johnny. "And who might you be?" he asked.

"John Chapman," said Johnny, shaking the old gentleman's hand. "Some people call *me* Johnny Appleseed."

"Is that right?" asked Dr. True. "Why is that?"

Johnny told him about his apple trees and about spreading God's word. He explained that he wanted to plant his trees in the wilderness for the coming settlers. When Johnny finished, he gently touched an apple on Dr. True's tree.

"The time will come," said Johnny, "when these settlements will be filled with trees as beautiful as this one."

Dr. True noticed Johnny's wagonful of seed sacks. "You have a heavy load there," he said. "Why don't you use a larger wagon and a horse? Then you can ride."

Johnny smiled. "I would not impose any work on an animal that I could do myself," he said.

Dr. True had never met anyone like Johnny.

"I'm about to have my dinner," said Dr. True. "Won't you join me? I'd like to talk to you some more."

"Thank you," said Johnny as he followed Dr. True up to the house. "You're very kind."

A middle-aged woman, her brown hair peppered with gray and partially hidden beneath a soft white cap, came into the dining room. She wore a pale gray dress, covered by a long, spotless white apron.

"Cook says your dinner is ready, Dr. True," she said.

"Mary," said Dr. True. "This is John Chapman. He'll be dining with me.

"Johnny," he continued, "I'd like you to meet Mary Lake. Mary's my nurse—and a very good one at that."

Mary paled slightly as she looked at Johnny's ragged clothes, bare feet, and long, stringy hair.

"Dr. True," she asked, "might I show the gentleman where to wash up?"

"Thank you," said Johnny. "I would like that."

Johnny followed her outside to the water pump behind the house, where he washed his face and hands.

"Now," said Mary, "you're ready to join Dr. True!"

Dr. True sat at the head of the table, waiting for Johnny. He pointed to the chair on his right.

"I'm happy you could join me," he said to Johnny. "We're having chicken and corncakes. May I serve you some?"

"Just some corncakes would be fine, sir," said Johnny.

"If you don't like chicken," said Dr. True, "we can fix you something else."

"Thank you, but I haven't eaten meat for the last few years," said Johnny. "I've decided it's wrong to take the life of a creature to feed your own body."

"You eat no meat at all?" asked Dr. True. "Not even fish?"

"Fish are God's creatures, too," said Johnny.

"Yes, of course they are," said Dr. True. He smiled at Johnny and gave him a large helping of corncakes.

All during dinner, Dr. True asked Johnny about his journeys through New York, Pennsylvania, and Ohio. After they finished their meal, they continued their conversation in the sitting room.

"I came to Marietta from Virginia when I was a young man," said Dr. True. "There weren't many doctors out here then, and I thought I could be of help. I, too, brought seeds—peach seeds and apple seeds—from my orchard back home. I planted them behind my house so I'd have fruit and seeds to give my patients."

He smiled at Johnny and continued. "So you see, Johnny, you and I are somewhat alike. But I never had your vision. It never occurred to me to plant orchards all over the wilderness!"

"Before I head out to the edge of the frontier, I'd like to start a nursery in Marietta," Johnny told him. "Do you know of any land I could use?"

"I have a friend by the name of Whipple," said Dr. True. "He lives in one of the buildings atop Fort Harmar. He might be able to help you. We'll go see him tomorrow. Why don't you spend the night here in the meantime?"

"Thank you," said Johnny. "But if you don't mind, I'd like to sleep under your apple tree."

Dr. True smiled.

"That's fine with me, Johnny," he said. "I wouldn't mind joining you myself. But my old bones couldn't take it!"

The next morning, Dr. True drove Johnny out to his friend's house.

"What brings you here, my friend?" Mr. Whipple asked Dr. True.

"Johnny Appleseed has given himself an important mission in life," said the doctor. "I thought you might be able to help him."

"There's some good land behind the fort that you can use," Mr. Whipple told Johnny when he heard of his plans. "When would you like to start?"

"If it's all right with you, sir," said Johnny, "I'd like to start right now."

"Fine!" said Mr. Whipple. "Why don't we all go over and look at the land together."

Dr. True, Mr. Whipple, and Johnny climbed aboard Dr. True's buggy and drove over to the fort. Johnny looked at the wide open field. "This is fine land for a nursery," he said.

After the others left, Johnny started clearing away the rocks and brush. Now and then, he drank from a nearby stream.

Several days later, five young men from town passed by

the field. They stopped and watched Johnny for a while. Then they offered to help him. From then on, whenever they could, they worked on the new nursery.

Johnny and the young men worked through the fall at clearing the land. They wanted to finish as much as possible before winter weather halted their progress.

Late one afternoon in early November, Mr. Whipple came to see how things were coming along.

"You're doing a first-rate job, Johnny," he said.

"Well," replied Johnny, "I have fine help, and you've given me good land. There's room here for a thousand apple trees!"

"When will you plant the seeds?" Mr. Whipple asked him.

"In the spring," answered Johnny. "My helpers said they'd like to care for the nursery and sell the trees for me after I leave."

"Fine with me," said Mr. Whipple.

He glanced at his pocket watch. "I have to go," he said. "I told Dr. True I'd drop by. Why don't you come with me? You look a little tired. Besides, it will be getting dark soon, and I assume even you don't work in the dark!"

"Thank you," said Johnny. "You're right—I *am* feeling a bit tired."

They rode into town in Mr. Whipple's wagon, and Dr. True greeted them at the foot of his path.

"What a pleasant surprise to see you, Johnny!" he said. "Come into the house."

"I'm feeling a bit warm," said Johnny. "Would you mind if we stayed outside for a while?"

"Not at all," said Dr. True.

Johnny sat down on the ground and wiped his forehead with his hand. "Dr True," he asked, "may I trouble you for a glass of water?"

"I'll get it," said Mr. Whipple. "You stay here with Johnny. He doesn't look so good."

When he returned with the water, he found Johnny collapsed in Dr. True's arms.

"Help me get him into the house," said Dr. True.

With Mary's help, they put Johnny to bed in a spare room.

"I'd better go," said Mr. Whipple. "Johnny needs your attention. I'll stop by in the morning to see how he is."

Later that night, Johnny felt no better. He had a fever and ached all over.

"I don't like the looks of this, Mary," said Dr. True. "He's developed a rash. I think Johnny has typhoid fever."

"Typhoid fever!" she whispered. "Do you really think so?"

Dr. True sighed. "I wonder where he got it," he said. "Typhoid fever usually strikes as an epidemic, so it won't be long before a lot of others will be sick, too."

The doctor patted Mary's shoulder. "I'm afraid we're in for a difficult time," he said.

Dr. True was right. In a few days, almost a third of the town had developed typhoid fever. A stream flowing into Marietta had been contaminated by flies carrying the disease; anyone who drank from it became sick, and many people died.

Johnny's condition grew worse. Most of the time, he didn't even know where he was. Thoughts whirled through his brain like wild winds. Sometimes he thought he was a little boy back in Longmeadow, running down the road in front of his house—first he'd run one way to the river, then he'd run the other way to the woods. Or he would think he was under-water saving Nat or in the snowy cave in Ischua. One minute Johnny was hot, and the next minute he was freezing cold.

Then, one morning a few weeks later, Johnny opened his eyes. He looked over to find Dr. True and Mary Lake standing next to this bed.

Dr. True immediately felt Johnny's head.

"Thank the Lord, Mary," said Dr. True. "The fever's broken. He'll be all right now."

In a few days, Johnny felt much better. But it took weeks before he was completely well. The terrible typhoid epidemic continued. As soon as he was able, Johnny helped Dr. True and Mary. For weeks on end, the three of them cared for the sick. They frequently worked straight through the night.

"When will this ever end!" said Mary.

"It will, my dear, in time," said Dr. True. "Everything comes to an end—even typhoid fever."

CHAPTER 11

By April, the epidemic was over and Marietta gradually returned to normal. There had been no rain that spring, and the grasses were stiff and dry. By late June, Johnny knew it was time for him to move west.

One morning, after packing his belongings, he went to a neighboring cider mill and collected several large sacks of seeds from the owner. Then he stopped at Dr. True's to say good-bye.

"It's time for me to move on," said Johnny. "I'd like to get started on more nurseries farther west."

"Well, why don't you at least stay until Saturday?" asked Dr. True. "There's going to be a cabin-raising for the Henderson family. I know they'd appreciate your help."

Johnny agreed to stay, and early Saturday morning, long before the sun was up, he joined dozens of families headed out to the cabin-raising, their wagons loaded with tools and baskets of food. The Hendersons' homesite was several miles out of town, past the fort and Johnny's nursery. The stream that flowed alongside the nursery also ran through the Hendersons' land. Because of the drought, the water level was lower than usual.

Long logs, smoothed and shaped into strong beams, lay on the ground at the homesite. There were almost one hundred of them, accurately cut to different lengths, waiting to become the walls of the Hendersons' log cabin. Nearby, chestnut wood shingles lay in stacks, ready to cover the roof.

"My boys and I cut those logs from black walnut trees," said Jed Henderson. "That wood's so strong my cabin could last for centuries." Then he laughed. "Too bad I won't last as long as that cabin!"

Jed pointed to an open field next to the stream and told Johnny, "I'm going to clear that land for an apple orchard. Folks tell me you just planted a nursery. I'll buy some saplings from there in the fall."

An old man wearing a wide-brimmed hat jounced up the road in a cart. He slowly climbed out and tied his horse to a tree. Johnny recognized him as a friend of Dr. True's.

"I'm William Johnson," the man said to Jed. "I'll be your raising master."

Jed shook hands with him.

"Much obliged to you," said Jed. "I've heard folks say you're the best raising master around."

"Well," said William, "I've had enough practice. Can't count the cabin-raisings I've been to. I may be too old to lift logs now, but I sure know *how* to do it!"

By five-thirty, the sun was up, and everybody ate breakfast, seated on benches placed by long tables. Hungry neighbors helped themselves to corncakes and maple syrup, sizzling bacon, and cups of hot coffee.

At six-thirty, William stood up. It was time to begin.

"Before we start," he said, "I think it's fitting that Johnny lead us in a little prayer."

Everyone quietly bowed their heads, and Johnny prayed aloud.

"Dear God in heaven," he said, "bless Jed and Margaret Henderson and their little ones as they begin a new life with us. May their house always be filled with love, health, and joy. Amen."

"Amen," said William softly, and then the cabin-raising got under way. First the men marked off the space where the house would stand. Then, swinging sharp axes, they chopped down trees and dug out stumps and roots. With shovels and hoes, they leveled the land, smoothing the dirt.

Finally, one of the men called out, "Ready to roll the logs!"

William stepped in, and under his careful direction, the men rolled and lifted one log after another into place. The work was strenuous and went slowly.

As the men worked, a light breeze sprang up, and the sky began to turn cloudy. Thunder rumbled in the distance, and lightning flashed on the horizon.

"Hurry up, boys," said William. "Maybe we can beat the storm."

The thunder grew louder, but no rain fell.

By late afternoon the cabin-raising was over. The cabin walls were up, and the heavy work was done. The Hendersons would chop out openings for the door, windows, and fireplace themselves. To keep out the cold air, they'd fill in the gaps between the logs with clay, grass, and small chips of wood.

Johnny and several other men rested under a tree.

"We're lucky," said Johnny. "The storm passed us by."

He looked across the horizon at the last flickers of lightning when something else caught his eye.

"Over there," Johnny said. He pointed far in the distance. "Is that smoke?"

"Good Lord, you're right," said one of the men. "The lightning must have started a fire—and the wind's blowing it this way!"

The man sprang to his feet. "Fire!" he shouted.

As soon as he heard the words, William took charge again.

"We'll have to build a firebreak," he said, "and try to stop it here. Just pray the wind doesn't shift. If the fire heads toward town, we could lose Marietta!"

Johnny ran up to William. "I'll go into town for more help," he said. "And I'll also get more supplies for fighting the fire."

"Good," said William. "Take my horse—we'll get started digging a firebreak. If we can clear away everything the fire can burn, it won't move forward."

Johnny unhitched William's horse and rode the galloping animal straight to the town's general store. Inside, Johnny found the owner, George Ketcham, standing behind the counter helping a customer.

"Hurry!" said Johnny. "A fire's heading toward the Hendersons' homestead, about five miles west of town. We need help and all the shovels, buckets, and old flour sacks you've got!"

"I'll ring the alarm," said George. "My wagon's out back. Start loading up!"

George ran down the road to the church and dashed up the steps. He pulled the long rope hanging in the belfry. The church bell loudly clanged the signal of alarm. Everyone in town dropped what they were doing and headed for the church.

"Fire, five miles west!" shouted George to the shopkeepers and townspeople running toward him.

Behind the general store, Johnny finished loading George's wagon and hitched up William's horse.

"Wait for us!" shouted George. He and four other men scrambled into the wagon. Johnny shouted to the horse, and they were off. As he drove out of town, people on horseback and in wagons followed closely behind him.

When Johnny arrived, he could see men in a long line that stretched across the field, digging a wide trench in the path of the fire.

Johnny's passengers each grabbed a shovel, jumped down from the wagon, and dashed over to help the men at the firebreak.

The horizon glowed with the setting sun and the fast-approaching flames. Even though the fire was still a few miles off, the air had already grown thick and smoky.

"How are things going?" Johnny asked William.

"The firebreak's still far from finished," William said, "and the fire's moving in fast. I hope you brought plenty of buckets—this place has got to be soaked down."

"I've got a whole wagonload of buckets and sacks," said Johnny. "And there will be a lot more people here in a few minutes."

"Good work!" said William.

Women ran to the wagon, grabbed buckets, and hurried to fill them in the stream. Then they ran to dump them out along the entire length of the firebreak.

"That's it," William called. "Soak the grass good. Thank goodness the stream didn't dry out in the drought! If the firebreak's not finished before the fire gets here, maybe the wet grass will stop the flames. Hurry now!"

The sun sank below the horizon, but the fire lit up the night sky. The women continued to soak down the grass while the men worked furiously on the firebreak. An hour later, the firebreak was finished. It was five hundred feet long and thirty feet wide.

"You've done a good job," William said to the exhausted men. "It should be wide enough to stop the fire. But then, I've seen plenty of fires jump right across firebreaks."

A gusty night wind picked up as the fire came closer. With each passing minute, the roar of the approaching flames grew louder and the smoke got thicker.

"I don't like all this wind," William said to Johnny. "It could spread sparks real fast."

"I think we'd better get those flour sacks out right now," said Johnny.

He ran over to George's wagon and brought back an armload of sacks. Then he quickly handed them out.

"What should I do with the flour sack?" asked a young woman. "I've never fought a fire before."

"Get it dripping wet in the stream," said Johnny. "When it's windy like this, sparks can fly all over and start new fires. Wherever you see a spark, beat it with the wet sack."

The young woman's eyes grew wide. "So even if the firebreak works, sparks could still set fire to this whole place anyway?" she asked.

"That's right," Johnny said. "But if we watch the sparks carefully, then maybe we'll stop it from happening."

The young woman nodded. Then she took two sacks from Johnny.

"I'll wet one for you," she said.

"Thank you," he said. "Now let's hope we don't have to use them."

Johnny walked over and stood next to William. The fire was only minutes from reaching the firebreak. Everybody watched from a safe distance and held their breath as the first edges of the fire reached the firebreak. When the flames touched the wet grass, they sputtered and died out.

William held up his crossed fingers. "Things look good," he whispered to Johnny. "Things look really good."

But the old raising master had spoken too soon. The wind tossed flying sparks across the firebreak. They landed in a patch of tall grass and set it on fire.

Johnny and several others ran over to the burning grass. Vigorously swinging the dripping sacks, they beat out the spreading flames.

"The wind's dying down," Johnny called over to William. "Now you're right—things do look good!"

After two more hours, the fire had died out completely, and everyone could go home to bed. William walked over to Johnny, who was kneeling at the moonlit stream and washing soot from his arms and face.

"You're welcome to spend what's left of the night at my place," William said.

"Thanks," said Johnny. "But I'm moving on tomorrow, so I'd like to spend my last night at the nursery, sleeping under the stars."

At sunrise, Johnny awoke to find a gray shape moving quietly along the stream. It was a young wolf.

Johnny propped himself up on one elbow and watched as

the animal quietly drank at the stream. He could see that the wolf was limping badly. He wondered if it had been hurt in the fire.

Johnny called softly to the wolf. It stopped drinking and looked up. Johnny called again. The wolf began to limp away, but then it stopped and turned its head toward Johnny.

"That's it," said Johnny in a quiet voice. "I can help you." He held out his hand, and the injured animal slowly came nearer.

Johnny stayed perfectly still, and as the wolf approached, he could see that its leg had been severely burned. When the animal was several feet away from Johnny, it stopped. Then it stretched out on the ground.

Careful not to make any sudden movement, Johnny got to his feet and slowly walked over to the wolf. The animal didn't seem afraid, so Johnny sat down next to it. For several minutes, neither the wolf nor Johnny moved. Then Johnny slowly put out his hand and stroked the wolf's head.

In a few minutes, the animal let Johnny look at its burned leg. After a short while, it let Johnny pick it up.

Trying not to cause the animal any more pain, Johnny carried it carefully into town and went straight to Dr. True's house.

"What do you have there, Johnny?" Dr. True asked. "A sick dog?"

"No sir," answered Johnny. "An injured wolf. He burned his leg in the fire. I thought we might be able to fix him up."

Dr. True stepped back a little. "A wolf?" he asked nervously.

"Yes," said Johnny. "I thought I'd build him a pen behind your house and leave him here with you. When he gets better, you can let him go back to the wild."

"Johnny," said Dr. True, "If word got out I was keeping a wolf behind my house, that animal wouldn't last five minutes. Folks around here don't think kindly of wolves—wolves attack their farm animals. This wolf would be shot by somebody at the first available opportunity."

"Who's going to know that the wolf's here?" asked Johnny.

Dr. True smiled and patted Johnny's shoulder.

"Johnny," he said. "The truth of it is I don't wish to treat a wolf. I know you love all of God's creatures, but I'm not the man you want."

Dr. True pointed to an old, large wagon parked beneath a tree in the yard.

"You can have that wagon," he said to Johnny. "The wolf can ride in it along with your sacks of seeds. It's the least I can do for not looking after him myself. But be careful, Johnny. Don't forget that this wolf's a wild animal, and he could be dangerous."

"All right," said Johnny. "I'll take him with me. But first, will you help me fix his leg?"

Dr. True hesitated, but only for a moment.

"I suppose so," he said. "Bring him inside."

Johnny carried the wolf into Dr. True's kitchen. He laid the injured animal on the floor, and together, he and Dr. True bathed and treated the wolf's leg.

Then Johnny said good-bye to his friend.

"I'll be back in a year or so to check up on my nursery," said Johnny. "If it's God's wish, we'll see one another then."

Dr. True handed a large box to Johnny. "These are for you," he said. "The general store just got in a supply. I thought you could use them; they'll keep you warm."

Johnny opened the box and lifted out a pair of expensive polished black leather boots. They certainly would keep him warm, but he couldn't accept such a costly gift. Dr. True had already done enough by caring for him and sharing his house. Johnny felt he couldn't take anything more from his generous friend.

"You're very kind," said Johnny. "But I can't take these boots. They're much too fine for me."

"You're just about the finest fellow I know," said Dr. True. "If they're too fine for you, they're too fine for anybody."

Johnny was so touched by the doctor's praise that he found it hard to find the right words to thank him. So he smiled, simply said, "Thank you," and put on the boots.

Then Johnny picked up the wolf. Dr. True opened the kitchen door for him and followed Johnny into the yard. He watched Johnny gently put the wolf into the wagon.

"Would you watch him for a minute?" asked Johnny. "I've got to get my sacks of seeds from the side porch."

"All right," said Dr. True. "But please, don't take too long!"

CHAPTER 12

Johnny walked slowly across the Ohio countryside, pulling the wolf and the sacks of seeds in the wagon behind him. After two weeks, the wolf's wounds healed, and the animal no longer rode in the wagon but trotted beside Johnny like a pet dog.

Late one night, while Johnny and the wolf rested in the woods, they heard the distant howling of a wolf pack. As the cries grew closer, Johnny's companion pricked up its ears and listened.

Johnny gently patted the wolf. "It's time for you to go," he said. "Go join them."

The wolf looked at Johnny as if it understood. After listening for a second or two more, it ran off and disappeared among the moonlit trees.

All the next day, Johnny followed a worn and deeply rutted wagon trail. At sunset, he looked around for a place to spend the night. Suddenly a man's loud voice broke the silence: "Come on! Push when I say push!"

"I am, Pa, I am!" a boy's voice said in return.

Next, a woman's voice reached Johnny's ears.

"Be careful, Harry," she cried. "I think it's going to tip!"

Johnny followed the sounds of the voices. Around a bend in the trail, he saw a large covered wagon. One wheel was stuck in the mud.

A worried-looking woman and three excited little children peered out the back of the wagon. They watched a barefoot man and boy slip and skid in the mucky ground as they struggled to push the heavy wagon. The wagon leaned dangerously to one side.

Johnny ran up to the man.

"Everybody should get out," warned Johnny. "It's too dangerous for them to stay in the wagon."

"I guess you're right," said the man. "Goshdarnit, this is the third time this has happened today. All right, Susan, you and the children get out!"

Johnny helped the family to free their wagon, and they invited him to have supper with them.

"We got swamped crossing the river yesterday," said Susan. "We lost our big trunk full of shoes and clothes."

"Susan and I aren't used to this life," said Harry. "We're city folk, but we have a great urge to live in this land and make it our home."

"Life out here is hard," said Johnny. "But once you pick some place to settle, you'll find your neighbors will be happy to help you."

Johnny told them a little about his plans for setting up apple orchards all over the Ohio Country. He took out a large handful of seeds from his sack and wrapped them in a handkerchief. "Plant these when you reach your new home," he said to Susan. "In a few seasons, you'll have your own orchard and all the apples you can eat."

After supper, Johnny led the evening prayers. Then the

tired family bedded down in the wagon while Johnny spent the night nearby. In the morning, before anybody was up, Johnny took off his new boots and put them in the wagon for Harry. He knew Dr. True would understand. Harry was a new pioneer. He needed the boots more than Johnny did.

Johnny looked at the clear morning sky. It was a good day for a walk. Once again, pulling his heavy load of seeds, he headed west.

EPILOG

Many stories of Johnny Appleseed have been told. Some are fact, others are fiction. It's often hard to tell one from the other. The stories in this book are a little of both.

John Chapman was born in Leominster, Massachusetts, on September 26, 1774. Massachusetts was the first state in America where apple trees were grown. They were brought from England by early colonists.

Johnny was not quite two years old when America declared its independence from England. As Johnny grew, so did his country; the new government opened up more and more lands to settlers. In the early nineteenth century, Ohio and Indiana were rugged frontiers. In those days, they were thought of as the Far West.

For more than forty years, Johnny Appleseed traveled, mostly on foot, through the wilderness lands of Ohio and Indiana planting his nurseries and preaching. He knew all about the value of trees in the wilderness. Settlers needed many different kinds of trees for food, boats, houses, furniture, tools, dyes, and medicines. During spring floods, tree roots, holding tight to the land, prevented soil from washing away. In the summertime, leaves provided cool shade from the hot sun. And throughout freezing winters, burning logs kept families warm.

During the course of his life, Johnny made frequent visits to his many nurseries, pruning the trees and making sure they were well kept.

On March 10, 1845, Johnny Appleseed died at the age of 70 in Fort Wayne, Indiana. The day before his death, Johnny had traveled twenty-five miles to a nursery to mend a broken fence—he was afraid that straying wild cattle would damage the apple trees.

During his life, news of Johnny Appleseed's frontier nurseries spread all the way to Washington, D.C. After his death, members of the United States Congress spoke of John Chapman's great contribution to life in the American frontier.

General William Tecumseh Sherman once said of John Chapman:

> Johnny Appleseed's name will never be forgotten.... We shall realize more and more the value of the work he has done. We will keep his memory green and future generations of boys and girls will love him as we, who knew him, have learned to love him.